WAGON TRAINS HEADING WEST

Rachel Stuckey

PowerKiDS
press

Published in 2016 by **The Rosen Publishing Group, Inc.**
29 East 21st Street, New York, NY 10010

Developed and produced for Rosen by BlueAppleWorks Inc.

Art Director: T.J. Choleva
Managing Editor for BlueAppleWorks: Melissa McClellan
Designer: Joshua Avramson
Photo Research: Jane Reid
Editor: Jennifer Way

Illustration & Photo Credits: Cover C.C.A. Christensen/Public Domain; title page, p. 4 Albert Bierstadt/Public Domain; cover, title page, back cover (skull) Jim Parkin/Shutterstock; cover, title page (wood) Dagmara_K/Shutterstock; back cover background homydesign/ Shutterstock; background siro46/Shutterstock; chapter intro backgrounds rangizzz/Shutterstock; p. 7, 16-17, 23 Carlyn Iverson; p. 8 Edgar Samuel Paxson/Public Domain; p. 10 War Department. Office of the Chief of Engineers/Public Domain; p. 14 Hippolyte Sebron/Public Domain; p. 17 Newbold Hough Trotter/Public Domain; p. 18 Samuel Colman/Public Domain; p. 20 J.C.H. Grabill(library of Congress)/Joshua Avramson; p. 24 Alfred Jacob Miller/Public Domain; p. 26 National Park Service/Public Domain; p. 28 Zack Frank/Shutterstock

Cataloging-in-Publication-Data

Stuckey, Rachel.
Wagon trains heading west / by Rachel Stuckey.
p. cm. — (The true history of the Wild West)
Includes index.
ISBN 978-1-4994-1179-9 (pbk.)
ISBN 978-1-4994-1207-9 (6 pack)
ISBN 978-1-4994-1200-0 (library binding)
1. Frontier and pioneer life — West (U.S.) — Juvenile literature.
2. Overland journeys to the Pacific — Juvenile literature. 3. Pioneers — West (U.S.) — History — 19th century — Juvenile literature. I. Stuckey, Rachel II. Title.
F596.S78 2016
978'.02—d23

Manufactured in the United States of America

CPSIA Compliance Information: Batch #WS15PK
For Further Information contact: Rosen Publishing, New York, New York at 1-800-237-9932

CONTENTS

Settlers traveled to the West in covered wagons. Settlers sometimes traveled together in wagon trains.

What Is a Wagon Train?

The first explorers to go to the West went on foot or by horseback. Soon they found the best routes and created trails that large wagons could travel. From the 1830s to the 1860s many **settlers** traveled west to claim land for ranching and farming. These people were known as **emigrants**. Families and individuals headed west looking for opportunity.

Settlers needed to bring their own supplies for setting up their **homesteads**, so they traveled in large covered wagons. The trip was dangerous and difficult, so most settlers traveled together with other emigrants. The wagons traveled in a line, with one wagon following another. This became known as a wagon train.

A wagon train was like a moving town. An elected captain or a hired guide led the train. The settlers worked together to cross rivers and hunt along the trails. They also camped together at night.

In 1803, the United States bought land from France in the Louisiana Purchase. This added territory to the United States stretching from the Mississippi River to the Rocky Mountains. At the time, Americans traveled from the East Coast to the West Coast by ships that had to go all the way around South America. This was a journey that took months. After the Louisiana Purchase, President Thomas Jefferson sent Meriwether Lewis and William Clark to explore the new territory and chart an overland route to the West. After the Lewis and Clark expedition mapped the Louisiana Territory, fur trappers and traders were first to move west. Many of these men lived among the Native Americans who already lived there.

Many others soon followed. People traveled to the West for many reasons. Some were looking for adventure, others wanted farmland. In the early 1800s, the **Great Plains** was not the farmland it is today. The grasses were too high, the land was too dry and too hard to plow, and there were not enough trees to build barns and houses. So the first settlers traveled across the Great Plains to the better farmland of California and Oregon.

Jedediah Smith

Jedediah Smith was born in New York in 1799. In the 1820s he went to Missouri to join William Ashley's trading expedition to the West. He faced many dangers on his journeys, even surviving a grizzly bear attack. For most of history, Smith's role in exploring the West was forgotten. But he was the first white man to travel overland to California. Along the way, he discovered the South Pass across the Rocky Mountains in today's Wyoming. This made it much easier for wagons to cross the mountains to Oregon and California.

Western emigrants began their journeys west in Missouri. They traveled along trails identified by early explorers and pioneers. Some settlers stopped along the trails and set up forts, missions, and trading posts. Others traveled all the way across the Great Plains, two mountain ranges, and high deserts, to reach the fertile lands out West.

The Lewis and Clark expedition first mapped the lands where the Oregon Trail would later be established.

The Oregon Trail

The Oregon Trail is the longest and the most famous of all the wagon train routes. The 2,200-mile (3,500 km) route went from Independence, Missouri, across the Great Plains and through two mountain ranges to the valleys of the Oregon Territory.

The Oregon Trail was first established after Lewis and Clark explored the Louisiana Purchase territory, mapping the lands from Missouri to the Pacific Ocean. They were able to accomplish this thanks to the help of the Native Americans they met along the way. After more exploration of Lewis and Clark's route by fur traders, a route that could be traveled by a wagon was carved out. Additional routes were added, such as the California Trail that branched off the Oregon trail at Fort Hall, a **Hudson's Bay Company** trading post.

From the 1830s until the completion of the transcontinental railroad in 1869, around 400,000 people traveled the Oregon Trail.

The trip from Independence, Missouri, to the Willamette Valley in Oregon took four to five months.

The Route

In 1836, the first wagon train took the Oregon Trail to Fort Hall in the Oregon Territory, which is now Idaho. A few years later, the trail was cleared all the way to the Willamette Valley in Oregon. The first wagon train arrived in Oregon in 1841.

The Oregon Trail was not a single route. There were many starting points in towns in Illinois, Missouri, and Iowa. The trails came together in the Platte River Valley in Nebraska at the base of the Rocky Mountains. Wagon trains crossed the mountains through the South Pass, which is a wide prairie between the central and south ranges of the Rocky Mountains. At Fort Hall, the settlers could trade for new supplies before finishing their journey.

From Fort Hall, the Oregon Trail headed north and then crossed the Cascade Mountains into the Willamette Valley. Wagon trains started in May so that they could make it across the Cascade Mountains before winter arrived.

Year after year, the Oregon Trail was improved. **Cutouts**, or alternate routes, were created. Some people even set up ferries and bridges at river crossings and charged the wagon trains for this convenience.

Jesse Applegate

Jesse Applegate was a leader of a large wagon train known as the **Great Migration of 1843**. Applegate's group left their wagons at Fort Nez Percés and traveled by boat down the Columbia River. But one boat capsized and Applegate's son and another boy died. Later Applegate found a safer overland route known as the Applegate Trail. Applegate later helped to form the first government in Oregon.

MYTH: Wagon train settlers were poor farmers.

TRUTH OR MYTH? This is a myth. Joining a wagon train was very expensive. The wagon and **oxen** cost $400. Supplies for the journey cost another $1,000. More money was needed for tolls, fees, and replacement supplies along the way. Homesteaders also needed to buy supplies to survive their first winter in Oregon or California as settlers. Many sold their lands, household items, and even family **heirlooms** to pay for the trip.

The California Trail

At Fort Hall, settlers also could choose to take the California Trail. The California Trail was a collection of several routes south and over the mountains to Sutter's Fort in California. A journey on the California Trail was difficult. No matter which route they took, settlers had to cross the Forty Mile Desert of the Lahontan Valley in today's Nevada. It took two days to cross the desert in hot and dry conditions with no fresh water. Many animals and settlers died in the crossing. After the desert, settlers had to cross the snowy Sierra Nevada Mountains before arriving at Sutter's Fort near what is now Sacramento, California. After gold was discovered near the fort in 1848, the California Trail became the most popular choice for settlers. In the Gold Rush of 1849, 25,000 people went to California in wagon trains. That is more than 15 times the number of people who traveled to Oregon that year.

The Road to Salt Lake City

The **Mormons** were a new Christian group who faced discrimination. They hoped to build a new city for themselves. The Mormon Trail began in Nauvoo, Illinois, and ended in Utah at what is now Salt Lake City. For 20 years, thousands of church members made their way West on the Mormon Trail. Many Mormon settlers could not afford horses or oxen, so they pulled their own handcarts instead of covered wagons.

The Southwestern Way

The Santa Fe Trail was a trade route based on an old trail used by Spanish explorers and traders. It began in Independence, Missouri, and ended in Santa Fe, New Mexico. There the trail connected to the Old Spanish Trail to Los Angeles, California.

Many settlers traveled on steamboats on the Mississippi River to reach the starting point of a wagon trail.

Preparing for the Journey

Settlers began their journeys west from starting points in towns on the western frontier of Missouri. That meant they first had to find their way to the Mississippi River, either overland from the East or by river in a steamboat. Steamboats traveled on the Mississippi River to St. Louis, and then followed the Missouri River to Independence, which was the furthest west the steamboats could go. Settlers camped near the steamboat landing. A few miles away was the Independence town square, which was a major center of trade on the frontier. Newly arrived settlers would go to the town square to purchase the wagons, horses, livestock, and supplies they needed for their four-to five-month journey. In the 1830s and 1840s, Independence prospered, because it was at the beginning of the Oregon, California, and Santa Fe trails.

Most settlers traveled in ordinary covered wagons. The larger Conestoga wagons (inset) were too expensive.

Prairie Schooners

Emigrants needed large wagons that could carry all the things they needed for their journey and their new homes. These wagons also needed to be able to travel over rugged trails and in bad weather. Covered wagons were made of hardwood and had hooped frames covered in tough canvas. Because of their size and canvas tops, covered wagons looked like large sailboats from far away. That is how they got their nickname **"prairie schooners."** A schooner is a large ship with sails that was used for transporting goods in the 1700s and 1800s.

Conestoga Wagons

Most prairie schooners were ordinary farm wagons fitted with hoops for the canvas cover. The **Conestoga wagon** was a special kind of large covered wagon. The wagon floor was slanted on each side, which kept things from moving around. It was also designed to make crossing rivers and streams easier. Some settlers heading west used a Conestoga wagon, but regular farm wagons were more common. Conestoga wagons could transport loads up to 6 tons (5.4 metric tons). But because of their size and weight, they needed eight to ten oxen to pull them. That wasn't practical for most settlers heading west.

Oxen were the animals most commonly used to pull wagons.

Draft Animals

More than two-thirds of the wagons going west were pulled by oxen. Oxen were slow but strong and dependable. They were also much cheaper than horses or mules. Mules could make the trip two to three weeks faster than oxen could, but they were less dependable.

Almost no wagons were pulled by horses. Horses were much more expensive than oxen, and also needed more food. Settlers did bring horses though, as they were helpful for hunting and herding and scouting the trail.

Settlers also brought small herds of cattle on the trail. The cows provided milk along the way. But the settlers hunted wild animals for fresh meat so that they could save their cattle for their new farms in the West.

Supplies for the Journey

To survive for months along the trail, families needed to bring durable foods like rice, beans, dried fruit, **hardtack**, lard, bacon, cornmeal, flour, sugar, coffee, and tea. A family of four needed 600 pounds (272 kg) of flour, 400 pounds (181 kg) of bacon, 100 pounds (45 kg) of sugar, and 200 pounds (91 kg) of lard. Special kitchen chests contained all of the pots, pans, and other household items. Wagon trains also needed tools. Some tools were needed for the journey, such as shovels and axes. Other tools were needed for their destination, such as plows for farming and mallets and saws for building a cabin. Hunting knives, rifles, and shotguns were needed for protection and for hunting. Settlers also brought seeds for the crops they planned to grow. Many settlers tried to bring furniture and other things from home, but they often left them along the trail to lighten their loads.

Wagon train captains needed to be experienced with the trail on which they led settlers.

Life on the Trail

Before setting out, the different parties in the wagon train met and formed a government. One man was elected captain, and others were selected to help make decisions for the group. Sometimes wagon trains hired a guide who had more experience with the trail.

After they had finished buying supplies, each party of settlers carefully packed their wagons. Settlers were very careful not to forget anything. Once they began the journey, wagon trains couldn't turn back. It was very important to avoid delays. On good days, wagon trains traveled 12 to 20 miles (19 to 32 km) a day. But on other days, bad weather and accidents slowed them down. Little things like a broken wagon wheel could also cause delays. The wagons were so full of supplies that one or two people would drive the wagon and the rest of the party had to walk alongside.

MYTH: Circling the wagons was done during fights with the Native Americans.

TRUTH OR MYTH? This is a myth. There was a small risk that a wagon train could have their supplies or horses stolen in a raid by Native Americans. Arranging their wagons in a U-shape or circle at night was safer than camping separately. The wagons created a stockade to keep expensive horses safe from theft. It also kept oxen, mules, and cattle from wandering off.

Wagon trains traveled during daylight hours. Before hitting the trail at 7 o'clock, settlers had to wake up before sunrise for a simple breakfast of bread, bacon, and coffee. They also prepared food for their lunch. They then packed up the wagons and hitched the oxen. Those settlers on horseback would travel up and down the train to share information. At around noon, the wagon train stopped for a cold lunch and rest. The train started moving again at around 2:00 p.m. and traveled until 5:00 or 6:00 p.m. The wagons then formed a U-shape or circle for the night, secured the

Circling the wagons at night brought the settlers together to talk and share their fires.

animals, set up camp, and made dinner. Some settlers would sleep in their wagons or pitch tents, but many just slept on the ground wrapped in blankets.

The Teamsters

We usually think of wagon trains as carrying settlers west. But wagon trains were also used to bring supplies and information back and forth across the trails. The men who drove these wagons were known as teamsters, bullwhackers, or muleskinners. They were the only way to transport goods until the railroads were completed.

Native Americans rarely were a danger to settlers on the trail. The greatest threat was bad weather.

Dangers on the Trail

Weather was the greatest danger wagon trains faced. In the summer, the Great Plains had hot days, cold nights, and huge storms with rain, hail, and lightning. Heavy rains turned the trail into a river of mud and wagons and animals often got stuck. Crossing rivers was another great danger. Many people and animals drowned and supplies were lost to swift-moving rivers. However, the most common cause of death on wagon trains was disease. **Smallpox** and tuberculosis spread easily, and many water sources carried typhoid and **cholera**. Settlers also suffered from **scurvy**, which is an illness caused by not eating enough fresh fruits and vegetables.

Native Americans on the Trail

Old Hollywood movies often told stories of dangerous Native Americans who attacked white settlers. But attacks by Native Americans on white settlers were very rare. Some Great Plains tribes raided smaller groups to steal supplies and horses, but the danger was sometimes exaggerated so that settlers would buy more guns and hire protection for their journey.

Hundreds of thousands of people traveled west by wagon train. Accidents and disease killed about 10,000 people. But in all the years of wagon train settlement, only about 400 settlers were killed in conflicts with Native Americans.

In the early years most wagon trains made friendly contact with Native Americans. The two groups traded with each other, and wagon trains often paid tolls or small fees to pass through Native American territory. Later, as western settlement started to destroy the Native American way of life, conflicts increased and soon the Native Americans were fighting the United States Army to defend their land.

This 1869 photograph shows one of the last wagon trains passing one of the first trains on the transcontinental railroad.

The End of an Era

In the early 1800s, Americans traveled over water in ships that sailed the oceans and boats that traveled the rivers and canals. They traveled overland in stagecoaches, on horseback, and on foot.

To travel to the West, emigrants first had to travel to Missouri by steamship, riverboat, and stagecoach. By the 1850s, railroads had made the first part of the journey to the West easier, but settlers still had to join a wagon train, and endure another five to six months of travel.

In 1869, the first transcontinental railroad was completed. This railroad took seven years to complete and connected the network of railroads in the eastern part of the United States to the Pacific coast. On the train emigrants could travel from New York City to San Francisco, California, in about one week. The transcontinental railroad made wagon trains unnecessary because train travel was faster, cheaper, and safer.

Helping the Nation Grow

In the early 1800s, the United States territory stretched only to the Rocky Mountains. California and New Mexico were Mexican provinces and the British claimed the Oregon Territory. But settlers from the United States quickly began to settle the West. From the 1830s to the late 1860s about 400,000 people traveled west on the Oregon, California, and Mormon trails. This flow of settlers helped the United States claim Oregon from the British and New Mexico and California from Mexico.

Today's highways follow the same routes carved out by the wagon trains. Interstate 80

Scotts Bluff in Nebraska is a landmark that thousands of settlers passed on their way west. Today a highway follows that route.

MYTH: Once a wagon train reached its destination, the settlers' troubles were over.

TRUTH OR MYTH? This is a myth. Life on the trails was dangerous and difficult, but the life of a settler was also hard work. Settlers had to clear the wilderness before they could farm the land. And they had to build their own homes and survive their first winter before they could plant their first crops. It was possible to trade for goods at fur trading posts and military forts, but wagon train settlers mostly had to do everything for themselves. They worked hard to build the West.

travels across the Great Plains and on to San Francisco along the California Trail. Interstate 84 follows the Oregon Trail north from Idaho. These highways pass towns and cities that started as forts and trading posts along the trails. Today the trails are remembered with historical landmarks along the routes. In some areas you can still see the ruts left by the wagons or visit old forts where settlers stopped. These historic sites are protected to remember the importance of the wagon trains to American history.

Glossary

cholera A disease caught by drinking unclean water.

Conestoga wagon A very large type of covered wagon pulled by 8 to 10 animals.

cutout A shortcut or alternate route from the main trail.

emigrants People who leave their homes to move to a new country.

Great Migration of 1843 A wagon train with over 1,000 people that traveled from Independence, Missouri, on the Oregon and California trails.

Great Plains The large grasslands east of the Rocky Mountains.

hardtack Bread or biscuits that are hard and dry and last a long time.

heirlooms Valuable objects that have belonged to a family for many years.

homesteads Homes and other buildings on ranches or farms.

Hudson's Bay Company A British fur trading company that controlled the northern territories.

Mormons Members of the Church of Jesus Christ of Latter-Day Saints founded in 1830.

oxen Very large and strong animals related to cattle.

prairie schooners A large covered wagon that looks like a sailboat.

scurvy A disease caused by not eating enough vitamin C.

settler A person who goes into a new territory and builds a home to make a new life.

smallpox A deadly disease that causes fever and blisters.

For More Information

Further Reading

Domnauer, Teresa. *Westward Expansion.*
New York, NY: Scholastic, 2010.

Roza, Greg. *Westward Expansion.*
New York, NY: Gareth Stevens Publishing, 2011.

Todras, Ellen H. *All About America:*
Wagon Trains and Settlers.
New York, NY: Kingfisher, 2011.

Winters, Kay. *Voices from the Oregon Trail.*
New York, NY: Penguin Group, 2009.

Websites

Due to the changing nature of Internet links, PowerKids Press has developed an online list of websites related to the subject of this book. This site is updated regularly. Please use this link to access the list:
www.powerkidslinks.com/thoww/wagon

Index

A

Applegate, Jesse 11

C

California Trail 9, 12, 13, 15, 29
Cascade Mountains 11

F

farming 5, 19
Fort Hall 9, 10, 11, 12

G

Great Migration 11
Great Plains 6, 7, 9, 24, 25, 28

H

homesteads 5
Hudson's Bay Company 9

L

Lewis and Clark 6, 8, 9
Louisiana Purchase 6, 9

M

Mississippi River 6, 14, 15
Missouri 7, 9, 10, 13, 15, 27
Mormons 13

N

Native Americans 6, 9, 22, 24, 25
Nebraska 10, 28
New Mexico 13, 28

O

Old Spanish Trail 13
Oregon Trail 3, 8, 9, 10, 11, 15, 29
oxen 12, 13, 17, 18, 22

R

railroad(s) 9, 23, 26, 27
ranching 5
Rocky Mountains 6, 7, 11, 28

S

Santa Fe Trail 13, 15
Smith, Jedediah 7
Sutter's Fort 12, 13

T

trading 7, 9, 29

W

Willamette Valley 10, 11
Wyoming 7